The concept for this book was based on my nephew's visit to the emergency room. Both he and his parents had some questions and concerns about his visit.
I realized that for many parents and children, having an X-ray performed can be a stressful experience.
My hope was to share some helpful information about radiology with other children who may have the same experience.

This book is not intended to replace medical education, advice, or diagnosis by a health professional.

VIEWBOX™

Mission

Viewbox Holdings, LLC is a comprehensive group based on medical education, achievement, and scholarship. We are focused on the development of products and services to be used for the evolution of healthcare innovation.

It is our goal to introduce innovative experiences and educational resources into the world of medicine, as medicine can only be advanced through the sharing of information.

Children go to the doctor's office
for many reasons. Sometimes the
doctor has to take an X-ray to
see what's wrong.

This is a story about Ethan's experience getting an X-ray of his head. He shares his experience with his friend, Lula, during lunch.

Viewbox Elementary

While I was standing up in the swing this weekend, I fell off and bumped my head.

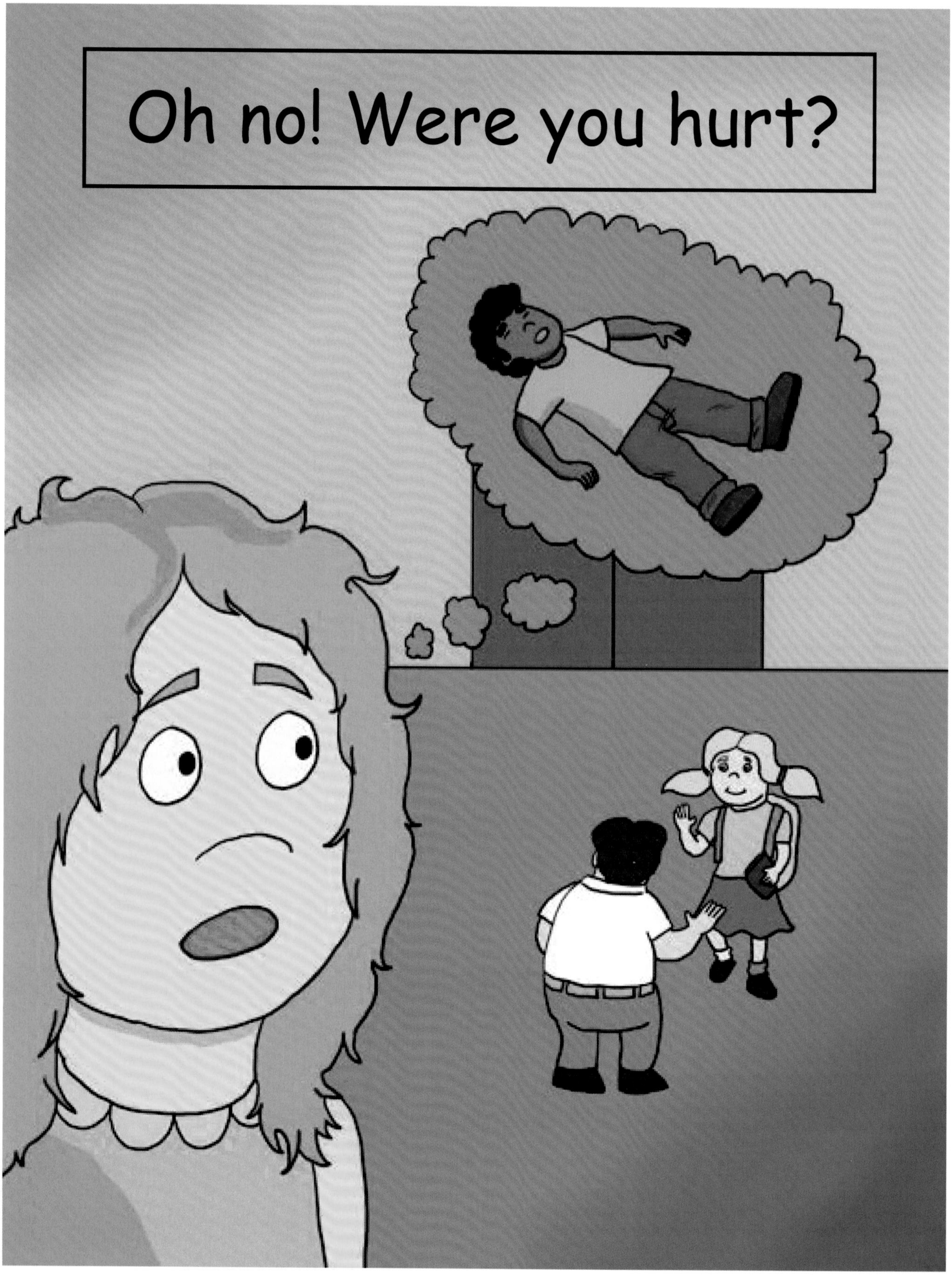
Oh no! Were you hurt?

Well, I didn't have much pain, but my parents took me to the emergency room. I got a picture of my head with a special machine that uses X-rays to see inside of our bodies. It was so cool that I was thinking about doing my science project on X-rays!

If you didn't have any pain, then why did you go to the hospital? What's an X-ray?

Viewbox Elementary

The doctor told me that sometimes we can get hurt inside of our bodies and not have much pain, so he wanted to get a special X-ray of my head called a CT scan.

Pediatrician

Learning Time!

X-rays (pronounced ex-rays) - are special pictures that allow a special medical doctor called a radiologist to see inside of our bodies.

CT scan (pronounced cee-tee) - is a machine that produces X-rays that allow a special medical doctor called a radiologist to see inside of our bodies.

No, because the doctor told me that my parents would be nearby when I had the CT scan taken.

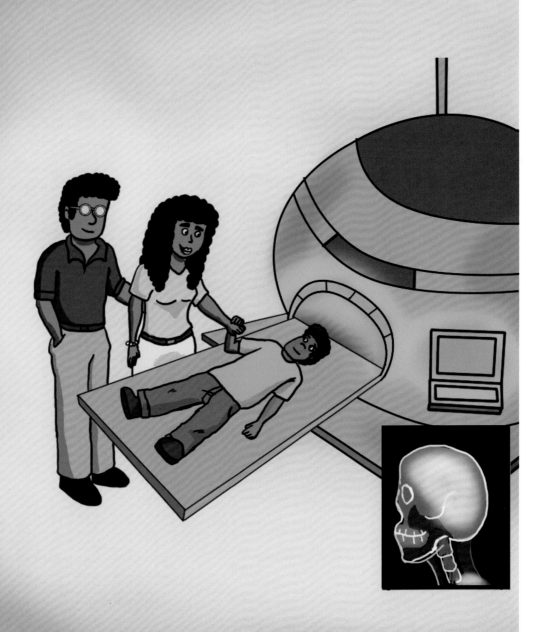

My doctor also told me that my parents and I could speak with a radiologist before we took X-ray to explain that it was safe.

Radiologist

Learning Time!

Radiologist (pronounced ray-dee-ol-o-gist) - A radiologist is a special medical doctor who can look at pictures created by X-rays that see inside of our bodies. These special medical doctors know how to figure out what is wrong with us by looking at these pictures. They are also trained to help answer questions about X-rays.

Yes, I had a special X-ray called a CT scan because I hurt my head.

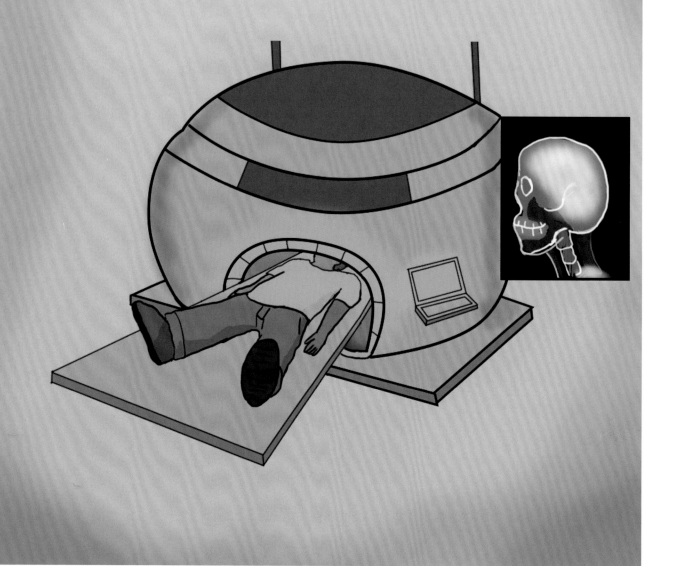

Because X-rays contain radiation, my parents said the radiologist will make sure they first try another test that DOES NOT contain radiation.

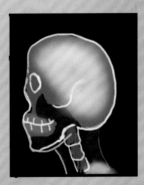

Radiologist

Learning Time!

<u>Radiation</u> (pronounced ray-dee-a-shan) - We get a small amount of <u>radiation</u> from an <u>X-ray</u> machine. The amount of <u>radiation</u> that we get flying all the way across the country is equal to about one <u>X-ray</u> of your chest. It takes a lot more <u>radiation</u> than one <u>X-ray</u> to cause injury.

The radiologist said that if you hurt another part of the body, he could find out what hurts by taking a picture with an ultrasound machine. He told me that ultrasound machines DO NOT use radiation, they use sound...kind of like a dolphin.

Viewbox Elementary

Radiologist

Learning Time!

Ultrasound (pronounced uL-Tra-Sound) - An ultrasound machine makes a picture of the inside of your body using sound, kind of like a dolphin makes pictures using sound. This kind of test DOES NOT have radiation. Sometimes a radiologist can use this picture to see whats wrong with you.

Radiologist

Learning Time!

Just remember that radiologists and your pediatrician want to help answer your questions and make sure get as little radiation as possible!

Notes

About the Authors

Luther B. Adair, II, MD

He is a board-certified, subspecialty trained radiologist
specializing in the diagnosis of abdominal and genitourinary illnesses. Dr. Adair is
a published author in the field of radiology. During his internship at Cambridge
Hospital and Harvard Medical School, he worked as a pediatric emergency room
physician. He is also a co-founder of Viewbox Holdings, LLC.

Seth Crapp, MD

He is a board-certified, subspecialty trained radiologist specializing
in the diagnosis of pediatric illnesses. Seth J. Crapp, M.D. is a member of the
Society of Pediatric Radiology and is a published author in the field of Pediatric
Radiology. With strong interests in Pediatric Radiology, Dr. Crapp undertook a
fellowship in pediatric imaging at Monroe Carell Jr. Children's Hospital at
Vanderbilt University. Dr. Crapp is a co-founder of Viewbox Holdings, LLC.

Please help us by completing a
2-minute survey about this book,
which can be found at

www.viewbox.net

For further information, please visit

www.imagegently.org